O9-AIG-757

To Grandpa Rueben, who showed me something will grow from all this...and it will be me.

TRISTAN Publishing, Inc.
2355 Louisiana Avenue North
Golden Valley, MN 55427

ISBN 978-0-931674-92-1
Printed in China
Fourth Printing

Hills, Jodi, 1968-
I'm not too busy / written and illustrated by Jodi Hills.

p. cm.
ISBN-13: 978-0-931674-92-1
ISBN-10: 0-931674-92-1
1. Time management. 2. Self-management (Psychology) 3. Conduct of life. I. Title.

BF637. T5H55 2007
650.1'1--dc22

2007027442

When we move so fast,

we

miss

so much.

Sometimes,

when you're not looking,

hours go by.

I could have gone for coffee with
the same friends I've cancelled on
three previous times,
but instead went to the post office early,
so I could avoid the traffic
and maybe beat the lines,
and still got held up
behind the accident
in front of me.

Sometimes,

when you're not looking,

days go by.

I encourage my microwave to hurry,
as I'm checking my e-mail,
and talking on my cell phone
to my friend who's in his car,
rushing to his next meeting,
and we're both worried that
time is actually speeding up,
but we can't get together,
because we're just too busy...

"So how does next week look?"

Sometimes,

when you're not looking,

weeks go by.

Calendars get filled,
and we have meetings
to set the next meeting,

and lives are penciled in,
easily erased by the next big event.

Birthdays are belated.

Children become adults

and grandparents' memories
are forgotten.

Holidays are celebrated

before and after

the actual date,

because they

just

don't

fit

in our schedules.

Hearts and families
are replaced with

"we'd really love to stay, but"

and

"hate to eat and run, but"

and

"I'd love to, but...

I'm just too busy."

Sometimes,

when you're not looking,

years go by.

We have to choose to slow down,
to actually see the time and space we're in...

to truly see people
and accept them
in their priceless moments.

Time isn't speeding up,

we are.

We have this urgency,
not to just get to places,
but to get there first...
even if it's just ahead
of that slow, red car in front
that's holding up all the traffic.

There's so much pressure
to pick the right line
at the bank,
or the grocery store,

and how dare they have 11 items
in the express line,
when you are nearing the 14th minute
of your 15 minute parking space.

Lines get longer
and tempers get shorter

and the only thing getting closer
is the end of our rope.

We even shorten words,
like thanx,
and luv,
as if shortening the word,
allows us to invest less energy, interest and time.

I'm not sure how much time we gain
by writing two less letters...
I'm certain someone has done the math,
created a study, and is now fighting
with someone else to prove or disprove
the figures...

But I **am sure** of what is lost,
by not taking the time,

to say the words slowly,

to write them out fully,

and to mean them with all that we are.

I need to stop and see things...

too many years have gone by.

To pay attention,
to notice people,
to care,
to have relationships,
to see the present,
to enjoy the given time
as a gift that is given -

that changes everything,

and slowly I begin to see you.

I do see you...

the smiling face that gets the thank you card,

the hand that waves as you let me merge into your lane,

the person alone on the bench,

the heart that feels joy,

the mind that seeks peace,

the fronts that belong
to the backs in line.

The tears.
the anger,
the frustration,
the glee,
the anticipation,

I see you.

We all want to be seen...

we all need to be acknowledged
for that moment in time...
that moment in time,
when you want to share your happy news,
or feel the warmth of an unassuming hug,
to let out the tears of a skinned knee,
to unload the frustration of hurt feelings,
or to rest your heart
in unjudging hands,

to look into someone else's face
and know
it's **more than ok** to be you...

we're all asking for a few precious moments,
and looking for someone to say,

"I'm not too busy."

Thank you,

thank you,

thank you, for seeing me...
even with all my
faults and distractions...

you do see me,
and
I loooooove that you do.

With all my limitations,
knowing that I can't reverse time,
save time, hurry it along, or slow it down...
I simply and humbly offer you a bit of my time,
which is really just a part of me.

If ever,

whenever you need me,

know, please know that

I'm not too busy.

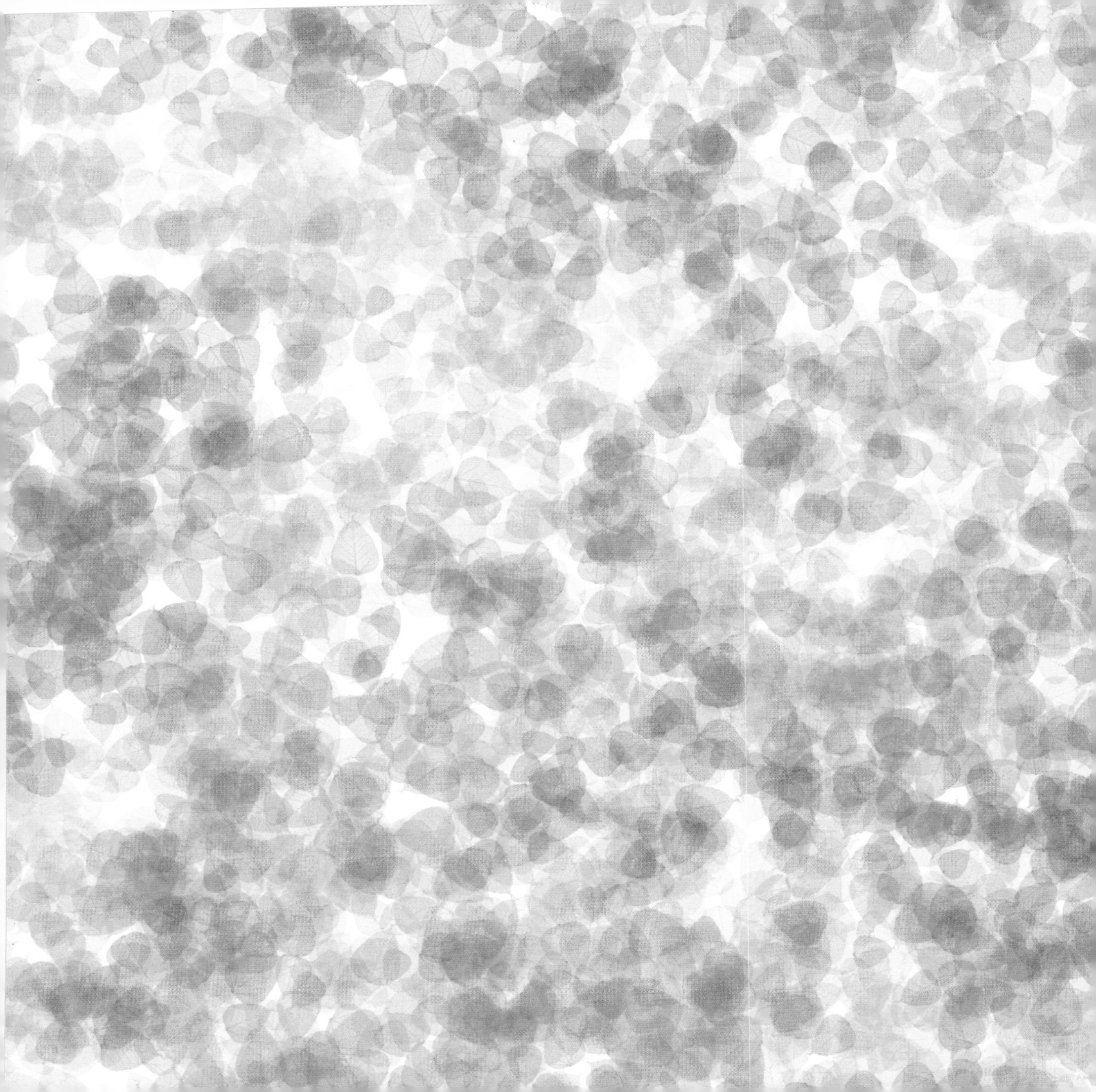